How to go No Contact With a Narcissist

Lauren Kozlowski

Published by Escape The Narcissist, 2020.

HOW TO GO NO CONTACT WITH A NARCISSIST

First edition. March 31, 2020.

Written by Lauren Kozlowski.

Table of Contents

Introduction: Why You Need to Go No Contact

Let me start this with a cold, hard truth. Your reaction to this fact will determine whether or not you are ready for the contents of this book:

In order to overcome a narcissistic relationship, there are two ways out: be discarded for the final time from the narcissist, or go no contact and cut yourself away from your abuser.

If you're ready to know all about no contact and are willing to give it your all in order to free yourself of your abuser, then read on.

Neither option is pretty, and I can't deny that both are painful. However, when you claim back your power by making the decision to go no contact, you give yourself the ability to leave the relationship with dignity, newfound self-respect and the makings of a solid foundation to build your future on. In stark contrast, if your abuser has left you high and dry with no explanation, effectively ending your relationship with one final heartbreaking discard, you will be torturing yourself with getting them back.

You'll be driving yourself crazy with thoughts about who they're with, what they're doing, and you'll be anxiously checking your messages and social media waiting for them to come back into your life. The upsetting truth may be that this could be the time they don't come back - this discard could really be the final one; they won't come crawling back as they have before.

I've been discarded more times than I can recall, and I know it hurts - the pain you feel when your abuser drops you quicker than you can realize what's happening is utterly crushing.

Even if you're in the discard phase right now, you can still go no contact. If your abuser has left and isn't refusing to speak with you, no contact is still an option - you can train yourself to stop getting in contact with them, and rewire your brain to focus on other things. Eventually, the trauma begins to heal. I can't say you'll ever forget how the narcissist has made you feel, but I can assure you that eventually, it won't have the same knife-in-the-heart reaction you once felt thinking about the abusive phases of the relationship.

I want this book to help guide you through leaving your abuser, if you haven't already done so, and finding the courage and resolve to be able to cut the narc out of your life completely with no contact. Scattered throughout this book will also be stories of survivors of narcissistic abuse who successfully went no contact, those who are currently trying to go no contact, and those who are struggling to stick to cutting the narc out of their life. This is to give you hope but to also show you that going no contact isn't as straightforward as you think it should be. There may be blips you may give in, but ultimately, that won't stop you from reaching your end goal of healing if you retain your determination to rid yourself of your toxic abuser.

I want to solidify in your mind exactly why you need to go no contact with the narc in your life. Chances are, after picking this book up and committing to reading it, you already know that you ought to be looking to sever the narcissist out of your life entirely. What's hard is actually putting this into action and sticking to it. You need to conjure up consistency if you are to really work through going no contact for good.

When I began looking at ways I could leave my abuser, and started seeking help on detaching myself emotionally from my abusive other half, I found myself overwhelmed; I truly didn't think I had enough strength to leave my partner. I was so codependent, believed I was in love with this person, and doubted that I'd ever meet anyone else ever again. More than this, I didn't *want* to meet anyone else. I was in the non-stop abusive cycle, and despite knowing what I needed to do, it took me such a long time to really put no contact into action.

During no contact, you shouldn't be initiating any kind of contact with your abuser. No phone calls, texts, Snapchats, Facebook messages, Instagram posts with them tagged, etc. You'll be tempted to text, call or reach out in the middle of the night when you're feeling the most alone and heartbreakingly vulnerable. Regardless of this, you must restrain, because there's a lot to gain from successfully carrying out no contact.

No contact provides you time for focusing on you and improving yourself and giving you time to properly reflect on the relationship and the events that have affected you so badly. It also allows you to get a more objective perspective on the abusive you've endured, which isn't something you could ever do whilst in the relationship. It'll allow you to eventually gravitate towards a more emotionally stable state.

You have a lot to gain by going no contact, and a lot to lose by skipping it. I want this book to be a tool for you to utilize, refer to, and come back to when you need a source of support through no contact.

Chapter One: How to Leave a Narcissist

So, you've decided.

You know you just can't live with the mental abuse and emotional torment of being in a relationship with a narcissist. In fact, you've probably known this for a while. But acting on this knowledge is hard - I understand. Leaving a narcissist is one of the hardest things you'll ever do. Getting out with your sanity intact may seem impossible, but it's not - you just need to make sure you're committed, consistent and understand that it will be hard (but ultimately worth it).

The first thing you need to do is leave your abuser. Much, much easier said than done, I get that, but it's not beyond your remit, regardless of your situation. I know financial situations, family circumstances, and stability play a big part in many victims staying with their abuser, *but you can still leave* - you just need to plan, prepare and be willing to give it your all when you finally execute your departure from the relationship. This is how I finally broke free from my abuser, and it's how almost every other survivor has freed themselves from an abusive relationship.

With all of the gaslighting, manipulation, nasty comments and constant battles, you'll already be emotionally and mentally exhausted, so leaving the relationship can feel like such an overwhelming thing to do. But you're reading this book, so your gut is telling you that leaving and cutting contact is what you need to do. I always tell people to trust their gut, and trusting your own instincts is something a narc tries to stop you from doing. As well as trusting your instinct, you need to make sure you have firm boundaries and remember at all times why you need to walk away.

Here's are the steps you need to take to make sure you can get out of this emotionally crippling, toxic situation:

Don't tell the narcissist that you're leaving them.

You shouldn't let on or outright tell the narcissist you want to end the relationship. As you know, narcs are manipulative and hate the idea of losing or being beaten at something, which is what they'd perceive you to be trying to do to them. Your emotional and physical safety is the priority through this, and even if you're tempted to throw the fact that you want out of the relationship into an argument, please think again before letting your heightened emotions get in the way of you preserving your safety.

Should you let on to the narc that you're seriously thinking about leaving them, don't be under the illusion that they'll be stunned into rethinking their treatment of you. Don't mistakenly think that they'll suddenly revert to their toxic ways and become the spouse they made you think they were at the beginning of the relationship. Your revelation about wanting to split from your partner will evoke one of two reactions, and both are fuelled by narcissism, manipulation and a fear of being 'one-upped'. Your other half will either love-bomb you into staying, making you feel adored, loved and needed by the narc.

They'll tell you how they can't live without you, how much you mean to them, and how devastated they'll be if you leave. This is often highly believable, and it pulls on our love for the narc and our abundance of empathy - which is precisely what the narcissist is banking on here. The crying, begging, promises of change, excuses, hurt expressions, and threats of what they'll do to themselves if you leave are all carefully crafted acts of manipulation from the narcissist. It can be very hard to comprehend this as the truth when you have a seemingly devastated person in front of you begging you not to leave them, but you need to keep this at the forefront of your mind if you've told the narc that you want out. The love-bombing exhibited at this point is a way to tap into your trauma bond with the narc; they know they've emotionally trapped you, and that leaving is hard for you. An episode of love-bombing can often keep the victim entrapped in the relationship, after which the narcissist will revert back to their toxic, hurtful ways.

The second reaction that you may be exposed to is the one filled with rage, injustice, and spite. The narc will be enraged by you wanting to leave them - *how dare you! You should know better than that - after all, you're lucky to have them! You'll pay for daring to think about leaving them!*

This is then the lead up to a bout of rage, which can be physical, verbal, or both. It's enough to frighten you into staying in the relationship. I know for me, particularly towards the end of the relationship, the outbursts of anger and aggression to anything my ex perceived as a threat were a big factor in me staying with him. In the earlier days of the relationship, I'd stay because I thought his behavior was excusable, because I believed his manipulation, and because I thought I could make him 'better'. When the abuse, rage, and manipulation engulfed me, the love I had for my abuser was drowning in codependency,

Aim to make copies of all your important documents.

This is an important step to remember, and one that lots of victims neglect to think about doing. And who could blame them? When you're in the throes of an abusive relationship, all logic is sapped from you. You can't think straight enough to even digest your own thoughts, let alone have a clear enough head to think matter-of-factly. In spite of this, in order to leave a narcissist, you need to get your house in order first, and make it so you're in a position to leave as swiftly, efficiently, and as safely as possible. Preparation before execution is something I highly vouch for.

I connected with a former victim last year who told me her abuser hid all of her documentation to stop her from ever leaving, should she muster the courage to do so. This was especially difficult for her, as she was originally from Poland. She had no friends or family where she lived with her abuser, and he'd also stripped her of her passport, leaving her stranded in a foreign country with him. She was essentially a prisoner in a country in which she knew no one and had nobody to turn to.

I've found it's highly common for a narcissist, both through personal experience and from speaking to other survivors, to hide things like this in order to thwart any attempts from the victim in leaving the relationship.

At the very least, I'd advise that you locate your personal documents, take some photos of them (or scan them using a scanner app on your phone), and send them to yourself via email. Get hold of everything you can, even things you don't perhaps think of as important, including proof of address, your bank details, all of your ID, and any official documentation. If you can get these original documents compiled and put somewhere safe, then that's the ideal scenario. If you can't, then copy as much as you can and keep it in a folder on your laptop, phone, or keep a physical folder of all your copies in a discreet place.

If your abuser has already got your documents and details and doesn't let you have access to them, you can either wait until they are out and make your copies then or tell them that you need your documents really quickly to fill out an application form. try to use this time to get your copies made.

Try and be in a position where you have some money saved or some spare cash.

Ideally, before leaving a narcissist, you ought to make sure you set up your own bank account. I know this may not always be possible, but you can open an account much more discreetly these days than in days gone by. You don't necessarily need to have letters confirming the account has been opened sent to your home, as there is the option to keep your account paperless on most accounts. If you can't open a separate account, then I'd suggest saving any spare cash you can - no matter how small - in a safe place.

In most cases, this might need to be done a bit in advance, just to make sure you definitely have your own money set aside. If the narcissist in your life is also a financial abuser, then you'll have to be diligent in how you do this, just so they can't use finances against you if they find out. This is undoubtedly a horrible situation to be in, but you can (and I believe, you will) climb your way out of this dark pit.

You don't need a whole heap of money set aside to leave, and the reason for saving may be different for each situation. In my circumstance, I was saving for a rental deposit, a couple of months worth of bill/food money, and a little extra if I could. If you have a job, then you can leverage that - perhaps do some overtime if you can or bump up your hours or offer to cover someone else's shift. If you don't have a job and rely on your abuser, then you have to do what you can do to build up your fund. One survivor I know secretly pawned her late mother's eternity ring to fund her leaving her abusive relationship. Luckily, she was able to buy it back, but it just goes to show the length some of us have to go to in order to be free. It's always upsetting to hear just what some victims need to resort to in order to claim back their basic right of freedom.

I hope you don't have to resort to extreme measures to fund your freedom, but I do believe that whatever it takes to break free from the relationship is ultimately worth it; you can come out of this and rebuild yourself. Maternal things, home comforts and keepsakes don't matter in the bigger picture. You can always buy new things, you can't buy more time. Don't spend your precious time in a surprising, abusive, manipulative relationship, and don't let the obstacles in your way put you off from leaving. Find a way to jump over those obstacles; failing that, go under them, around them, or if you have to, run straight through them.

Think about telling others what's happened to you.

I understand that you may not feel like you want to escalate the situation to the police, which I know many survivors can empathize with this feeling. Sometimes it's down to fear, to be afraid of being disbelieved, or because some victims don't understand the gravity of the abuse they're enduring. If you don't want to speak to the police, you should speak to someone. My suggestion would be to talk to your doctor. They're duty-bound to keep what you say to them within the four walls of their office, and they can offer you some helpful guidance, advice, and help you rationalize what you're going through.

From my own experience, I know it can feel daunting and awkward broaching this topic with your doctor. It can be incredibly difficult to know what to say or how to guide the conversation to your situation. You may find it less daunting to open up to your doctor with the line, "I need your help and I've been told I need to speak to my doctor about it. I'm in a relationship that causes me a lot of pain". They will guide the conversation in the right direction and offer you help with the side effects of abuse, such as anxiety and depression. Be open, be honest, and don't be ashamed.

Also, having this on your doctor's record helps you in the future if your abuser gets violent (or more violent than they already are, in some cases), or if you involve the police. Cover your own back as much as you can when you're planning to leave your abuser, even if it makes you feel uncomfortable.

Be diligent with what you stay logged in on a shared computer or device.

If you are someone who leaves yourself logged in to social media, banking sites, or leaves your computer or phone unlocked and unattended, then you're open to being tracked or checked up on by the narc. Likewise, if your abuser insists on knowing your phone password, or sharing the same computer profile, this is a sure-fire way for them to obtain and retain control of your movements. The abuser may even have more sinister intentions from knowing your details; I've spoken to many survivors who were stolen from by their abusive ex, or had credit taken out in their name by their abuser. Compile a list of everything you've signed into or entered your bank or card details into and make sure you haven't left them open or with auto-fill setup so your device remembers them all.

Also, if your abuser is anything like my ex was, anything that connects you to other people or allows you to see how other people are getting on, such as mobile phones or laptops, is frequently banished or smashed up. This means that there may be some instances where you're without these things, which can be vital tools for keeping you connected with reality and seeking out ways to keep yourself sane throughout the abuse. It also strips you of your ability to reach out for help.

If this is the case for you, I'd recommend an old phone to keep locked away and hidden. Just a cheap, older one that has a long battery life. Whilst it may feel deceptive doing this, which I know a lot of victims feel like when they 'go behind their partner's back' to do things like this, try to retain your rationale as to **why** you're doing this.

Would you still be having to covertly buy and hide a phone 'just in case' if you had an emotionally healthy, loving relationship? Would you be made to feel so bad and guilty about something like this if you were in a genuine, caring partnership? What kind of spouse would make their partner feel so frightened of them that they'd resort to this, anyway?

Be mindful of trackers.

This might sound like something out of a film, but you'd be surprised to hear the number of survivors who have been sneakily tracked by their abusive partner. You can buy car trackers online pretty cheaply, and there are remote-access trackers for phones, too.

If your phone is acting strangely, such as being slow or having a weak battery life, consider it suspicious. You might think this is the height of paranoia, but abusive partners seek out ultimate control. Knowing where you are and making you corroborate your whereabouts and where you say you were is something they take great joy in. If this doesn't match, they'll become enraged.

It doesn't have to be a direct tracker that you need to be wary of, either; in my case, my partner would access my Kindle from his phone, checking what I was reading and downloading. He could also check my internet search history. This was unsettling, as it felt nowhere was safe for me to read about abusive relationships or narcissism. I couldn't buy physical books, I couldn't search for blogs on our shared computer, I couldn't join abuse support groups on Facebook - my ebook reader was my solace, but he stripped that from me, too, for a period.

Remember, their flattery isn't real.

Narcs share a lot of the same traits and characteristics, and being deviously clever is something that you usually find in most narcissistic individuals. This is something you need to keep in mind when your abuser tries to keep you in their clutches with extreme flattery. When a narc sense that something is up, or that their grip over you is loosening, they'll try to combat it in one of two ways; either love-bomb you back into the relationship, or ramp up the abuse to create a world for you in which you fear leaving. They'll wear you down to the point where you'd rather be stuck with your abuser than try to endure a world where you've left them - you'd be too scared of their wrath to do that.

It's hard to comprehend that when your abuser suddenly reverts to being hugely flattering, full of love and adoration for you, that this is simply a manipulative tactic. When you're being love-bombed, the narc becomes all you've ever wanted them to be; caring, attentive, and 'in love' with you. Of course, as soon as you see this behavioral change from the narcissist, you drop all of your prior thoughts of leaving the relationship and are sucked right back into the abusive cycle. Without fail, when you're well and truly back under the spell of the narcissist, they'll revert back to their nasty, mean, cruel, and manipulative ways.

I know it's hard when you're being love-bombed to snap yourself back to reality, but it's a must: you need to remember that you deserve better than this, and you owe it to yourself not to get sucked back into their abusive cycle.

Try to reconnect with family members and friends.

Abusive narcissists often try to (and successfully manage to) cut you off from your friends and family, so it's understandable that you might not have seen some of the people who should be closest to you for quite some time. The manipulative narc may have even turned you against them by spreading nasty lies, purely because they hate the idea of you being around anyone else.

A really important thing to keep in mind is not to allow any shame, embarrassment or fear of how they'll react to seeing you prevent you from reaching out. It might also be a pride thing stopping you from getting back in touch, but if you go into this with a mindset of openness and honesty, you'll be pleasantly surprised about how understanding and sympathetic to your circumstances people are. I can't promise this is the case for *every* person you've lost or cut contact with, but don't let that put you off. You're creating a solid foundation for you to rip yourself out of your abusive relationship, and you can gain strength, courage, and motivation from those around you if you allow it.

In some cases, people may be shocked by the extent of the abuse you've been suffering. In others, they may have known but felt powerless to help, especially if they feared making things worse for you.

So, take a deep breath, think about all the people you used to be close with, and reach out. Be willing to explain your situation, understand that they might feel a little hurt by things too. Allow an open and honest conversation, and I think it will be quite cathartic for you. Should anyone shun your attempt to reconnect, don't let this put you off. It happened to me, too, and although it hurt at the time, it definitely helped me trim out anyone who was never a true friend in the first place.

Don't buy into the sob stories.

Remember: the narc will try to tug at your heartstrings to try and keep you.

They might offer what seems like a heartfelt apology, or offer you keepsakes that remind you of the nice parts of the relationship, or try to sweep you off your feet with some grand gesture. As nice as these may seem, remember that you're in an abusive relationship, and manipulation of your emotions is a big part of that.

Beware of this triangle of abuse, whereby the abuser can flit between being your hero or savior, to being your tormentor, to then acting like the victims themselves. This triangle will then be repeated as long as you allow it.

Make a list.

You need to be your own pillar of strength throughout this time, so if you need any reminder as to why you need to leave this abusive relationship, I suggest making a list of every bad, hurtful, mean, toxic, manipulative thing your abuser has ever put you through.

When you find yourself being sucked back in, read your list. Keep it somewhere handy, like your phone. Use it as a reminder that your warm fuzzy feelings towards your abuser are a product of manipulation. If someone loves you, they wouldn't have carried out the things you have on your list.

Read the list and use it to think to yourself, 'why do I put up with it?'

Chapter Two: How I Left My Abuser

I can't lie and say I woke up one day, decided to leave my abusive relationship and suddenly mustered up the will and strength to do it straight away. As you may know yourself, this is a process: you don't go from beaten down and detached from reality to suddenly waking up one day and fleeing the relationship without looking back. More than this, even when I came to terms with the fact that I was in an abusive relationship, I didn't want to leave my abuser. I couldn't imagine life without him, despite my life with him being unbearable. This is a paradox that most people will never understand, but it's a common theme for those of us who have endured a narcissistic relationship.

It took me a good few attempts to leave for good. The first few attempts were admittedly feeble: I'd physically leave, but remain open emotionally by not blocking him and keeping in touch with mutual friends. Looking back, this was a way for me to know what my ex was getting up to, and to leave the door open for reconciliation. It was a misguided attempt from me at trying to make my ex see that he could lose me without really losing me. A lot of the time, it was me who got back in touch in order to reconcile.

It's safe to say those first few no contact attempts fell flat, and only served to cause me lots of anxiety for nothing: I knew I didn't really want the relationship to end.

It was only when the abuse escalated to heights that shocked even me - bear in mind, my ex put me in the hospital a few times, and I still went back to him straight after being treated in A & E - that I decided that I needed to leave for good. The abuse became something out of a never-ending nightmare, and I knew it was only going to end if I put a stop to it. I had two ways to do this: end the relationship, or to put it bluntly, end myself. I did come close to ending my own life a few times, but I still had a glimmer of hope in me that *life can be better*. Even at my lowest, hope always seemed to appear just when I needed it to. I would close my eyes and imagine a beach in the Maldives and picture myself living there without a care in the world. I would escape to this location whenever things got too much, and it afforded me that speck of hope that I needed to keep trying for myself.

It's only when you find the resolve inside you that you can really, properly leave. You need to start the fire inside you that fuels your ability to leave - and stay away. This fire doesn't engulf you overnight; you need to start with the kindling. For me, the 'kindling' was coming to terms with how cruel my abuser was, how badly mistreated I'd been, and how that had impacted my life and mental health. The lighter fluid was provided by the support and advice from other survivors from online groups. This was further propelled by the countless books, articles and blog posts on the topic. These things helped affirm that I wasn't crazy or deserving of such abuse. I was finally able to light the match and throw it on the kindling when I equipped myself with an abundance of understanding on the subject of narcissistic abusers. Now I was enlightened, knowing exactly what kind of abuse I was enduring, and I knew what I needed to do: I needed to leave.

As I mentioned before, the abuse was escalating to become more and more hurtful and manipulative, and I knew it was only a matter of time before I'd be ground down to the point of no return. I knew I had to first mentally prepare before I physically left. This was the advice that was given to me from other survivors that I'd connected with online, and it also afforded me the valuable time I needed to prep for the upcoming chapter in my life: one that would be without the person I cared so much for, my abuser.

This new chapter would be hard at first, full of yearning, heartbreak, upset, doubt, and rebuilding. However, it would also be full of promise. A life without abuse. Without being constantly berated, demoralized, manipulated, cheated on, or made to feel deserving of all things horrible. I could see, from talking to those that had walked this path before me, that through the painful stages of leaving your abuser, that a better life existed. As heart-crushing as it was to think I'd not be with the person I thought I would be with forever, I wanted more for myself. I wanted to feel at peace, not worried about what my spouse was up to when he didn't come home, or when he would next unleash his narcissistic rage upon me.

I slowly but surely built my escape plan, which was essentially a safety plan, and it was there to be utilized when I felt I was ready to leave the relationship for good. Steadily, I started to get my things in order. I photocopied all important documents and kept them safe in a drawer at work, alongside any important numbers and information.

I kept my passport somewhere safe, making sure I knew where it was at all times. I began putting some money aside where I could. My ex was extremely controlling with money, so I could only put aside a little here and there. It took around six months for it to add up to something substantial enough to be called a 'leaving fund', but saving what you can is a must - it may seem small at first, but it's encouraging to see the fund slowly growing. I also opened a secondary current account and made sure all statements and letters weren't sent to the house. I was also able to sell little things from around the house on eBay, which gave me a secondary little savings pot in my PayPal account, which was my back-up if my ex discovered I'd been stashing money away.

I also swallowed my pride and the sense of shame that had been instilled in me by confiding in my manager at work and letting her know what was going on. I felt comfortable talking to her as she'd always been supportive of me at work, and I do suspect she already knew I was in an abusive relationship. She was always very understanding of things with me, perhaps more so than she was with other workers. This, coupled with her lack of surprise when I told her about my abusive partner, makes me almost certain she already knew. One of the main reasons I told my manager was in case things escalated and I needed people to know I'd spoken up about the abuse previously. I had a huge fear of not being believed about the abuse if things had to come out, and this was one of the reasons I stayed in the relationship as long as I did. So, I aimed to combat this and overcome another fear of mine: to speak to others confidentially about the abuse I was enduring.

Before I opened up to my boss, I was unbelievably nervous; I was scared of being judged, of her opinion of me being changed for the worse, of her thinking I was stupid and weak. Of course, I can now attribute those feelings to being instilled into me by my abuser. His manipulative tactic of making me feel deserving of his abuse and telling me I was pathetic had paid off for so long; I never dared open up to anyone about the toxic relationship. However, when I relieved myself of the burden of silence by talking to my boss, I felt an overwhelming sense of calm and strength flood over me. I knew that our conversation had to remain confidential, and I also knew if I needed to call upon her to recount the story of abuse I told her, she would.

As well as this, I began keeping a journal of the abuse - times, dates and a description of what had happened that particular time. This little A5 journal was kept in my laptop bag, where I knew it was safe. It came with me to work, and my ex never looked in it when I brought it home, unlike my handbag or purse.

I also was lucky enough to confide in an old friend about the toxic state of the relationship and we came up with a 'safe word' together. This would be sent to her if I needed her to come to collect me or call the police. The word was so random that, if my ex checked my phone, he would have no idea what it meant.

Fast forward another three months, the time had come. It might sound like a long time to prepare - in total I think I spent just under a year preparing to leave and mustering up the courage to do so - but the day came when I knew I had to get out. And, because I'd spent the time building a support cushion for myself, documenting everything I needed to, saving a pot of money to fall back on and enough evidence to feel believed, I was ready. I remember the feeling I had that day so clearly. I had my friend pick up my kids from school, and when I left for work that day, I didn't really go to work. I went to pick up the keys to my new place.

Of course, it was incredibly hard, just like everyone said it would be. My ex reacted like I expected he would: the manipulation, the threats, the flying monkeys and their messages of revenge... sometimes I did bite back. No contact isn't as black and white as leaving once and making no contact work right from the offset; only in a perfect world would that happen. However, this was the last time I left for good - I didn't return to the relationship again after this. There was a bit of back and forth texting before I blocked him, but this time would mark the very first time I left the relationship with every intention of staying out of it.

Of course, he stooped as low as using the children as a bargaining tool and a way to manipulate me from afar, and I'm so grateful they were of an age where they could see what he was doing and were independent enough in their minds to know what he was like.

Chapter Three: How to Implement No Contact

When ending a relationship with a narc, you may be shocked by the range of emotions and behaviors they will go through to get you back. It's important to remember that there will be no real ending to things or genuine moving on for them if the narc wasn't the one to initiate the breakup. You may be thinking to yourself, particularly when you're feeling weak or like you want to give in, 'why do they stay with me if they don't truly love me?' It can be very easy to trick yourself into thinking that the narc is still with you out of love, but I want to take a moment to give you the real reason the narc keeps you around.

That reason is **control.**

A narcissist feeds off the control they hold over others. When you live with a narcissist, there are a couple of things to remember: 1) You can't, no matter how hard you try or how good your intentions are, control a narcissist, and 2) You don't have to believe everything they tell you. When you believe and accept the belittling comments and demeaning insults, and respond to them, you are essentially handing control over to the narc. Each time this happens, as it always does, this will empower the narc and give them the green light to do it again and again.

When you go ahead and do the unthinkable by ending it with the narcissist, this loss of control they feel coupled with the narcissistic injury the abuser feels leads to your partner clawing you back into the relationship. I've mentioned this earlier on, but I just want to use this part of the chapter to give you guidance on how to prepare yourself for this.

Tactic #1: Gray rock

Your abuser thrives off of the supply you provide, and the excitement and ego-boost that it offers them, so make that vanish. The gray rock method is more often described for situations when you're unable to go no contact, but in this situation, it can be extremely useful in calming things down.

Let me explain this a little more: it means you become essentially a bore, as a person who doesn't stand out, as someone who merely blends in you are just like a gray rock among the enormous amount of others on the lakeside. This refers to what supply you offer to your partner and how you respond to their cruel ways.

A narc is naturally drawn to and excited by drama, so you can combat this by taking the thrill out of abusing you. When their content tap of supply is apparently diminishing, the narc may well begin to grow bored with you, and seek supply elsewhere. I'm fully aware that this very idea may send shivers down your spine, but in order to let the narc go and detach yourself, you need to really make a conscious effort to remove yourself emotionally from our abuser.

I understand that when you're trauma bonded, the mere idea of being apart from your abuser can make you sick to your stomach. Maybe you're enduring this right now, or perhaps you've been through this and you're desperately trying to commit to no contact consistently; either way, this chapter will be able to offer you some advice on how to wade through this difficult time and know that there's light at the end of the dark tunnel.

Tactic #2: Understand your own emotional triggers

During the time you've been involved with a narc, they've been working out and understanding what's important to you. They'll know what causes you to feel happy, scared, sad, and guilty... no matter the emotion, they'll have educated themselves on just what it is that brings out any given emotion. In a healthy, emotionally stable relationship, this would be fine; in fact, some partners would like their partner to know more about what makes them tick. Sadly, when a narcissist is faced with rejection, they will use their plentiful knowledge on what triggers your emotions to try and convince you to come back or stay with them.

Because of this, I do think it's a good idea to take a sort of mental inventory of the shared bonding experiences, loving things you may have said to the abuser, as well as any secrets or fears you may have revealed. Be under no illusion. This is not to reminisce, so don't allow yourself to get sucked into the 'idealization' persona you initially fell in love. At the same time, don't use this thinking time to torture yourself, or begin a bout of self-hatred or anger. This is merely a mental exercise to help you detach yourself and move on from an abusive partner. Keep that in mind. Your mental inventory will ensure you know what memories, events, or fears may be brought up by the narcissist, aimed to trigger your emotions and pull you back in.

Tactic #3: Identify your sources of support

As I touched upon earlier, this may be difficult if you've cut off friendships or ties with your family, but reaching out to them is something I highly recommend. I want to just mention it again here, but to add one additional point that is vital in your journey: be sure that your sources of support aren't people that you met through your partner. You want to avoid your abuser using them as a pawn to get to you when you're away from the relationship. On top of this, you want to avoid, as much as you can, from any information about you getting back to your abuser. If you use a mutual friend as a source of support and open up to them, you're leaving yourself wide open for the narcissist to have a 'spy' working for them and updating them on your new life.

Tactic #4: Know what to expect when you leave

And so the journey really begins. The planning, the mental anguish you've put yourself through, and the constant battling with your logic comes to a head here. The more you think about what the narc will do, or try to do when you leave, the better you can prepare for it and avoid it. Telling someone you want to end a relationship is hard enough, but when you tell a narcissist - it can feel like a kick to your stomach just thinking about telling them it's done.

When I fled my abuser, I didn't hang around to give them my reason why or let them know I was going. I'd been planning it for a while. I'd squirreled money away, let someone at work know what was going on, I'd found a new place to stay and had things in place to ensure the abuse was documented. I left one morning, leaving the only world I'd known for so long, afraid, fearful, but with the understanding that I **had** to do this.

My advice is to leave in such a way that they can't stop you. You don't owe an explanation, you don't deserve to be made to feel guilty. Know that your partner will persist for answers, and try to reel you back in. Expect it. Depending on your abuser, your safety may be at risk, which is why I vouch for leaving when your abuser is gone and out of your way.

Tactic #5: Walk away and close the door behind you

If you absolutely have to tell your abuser to their face that you're leaving, I suggest you take on the broken record approach. Think of an old vinyl album with a persistent scratch–when it plays, and the needle hits that scratch, the same part of the song will play repeatedly. By adopting this mentality, you'll repeat your statement calmly, without getting flustered, over and over. This is a technique to be utilized when someone is trying to convince you or persuade you to do something, or if they're trying to knock your train of thought or get you rattled.

After you've made your point for the last time, end the discussion. This is where no contact begins.

Tactic #6: Understand that you'll now be in recovery.

Just like recovery from substance abuse, abstinence is key. If you allow there to be continued contact with the narcissist, you will undoubtedly remain in the abusive cycle. This consists of reuniting with the abuser–being love-bombed during the brief honeymoon period–old patterns reemerge and the abusive, toxic side of your partner is unleashed again–another break up occurs–and repeat. You've probably heard this before, particularly if you frequently reconnect with your abuser, but this will go on only as long as you allow it to. Before I went no contact for good, I would tell myself that I would be 'friends'; with my ex, for the sake of family and to make our lives easier. I was kidding myself, trying to find excuses and hold off on finding the strength to go no contact. Invariably, this 'friendship' always spelled the beginning of the abusive cycle, kicking in again.

With all of this in mind, I want to now go through the steps to take in order to keep the door closed once you've walked out of it.

First and foremost, ignore all attempts at communication. No matter how they attempt to get in touch, you must ignore it. By even creaking that door open just a fraction can put you back into the abusive cycle. Like a gambling addict with a slot machine, a little reward will encourage them to keep putting money in the machine, time and time again. If the gambling addict knew that they'd never receive any reward ever again, they'd give up. It's the same with the narcissist.

Now, I want to give you a 'no contact to-do list'. This is practical, logical, and a necessary step if you want to be free of the abuse and give yourself the chance you deserve to heal. I understand that the steps I'm going to advise you to take are hard, but they're without a doubt, actionable. You need to remember why you're here; why you're reading this book. Why you sought this book out (or books like this one). Why you felt the urge to seek out information on this topic.

Reaffirm with yourself just exactly what you want, and remember that you deserve a life free of toxicity, lies, manipulation, put-downs, and abuse. With that at the forefront of your mind, let me give you the must-do-to-do list that will begin your journey towards healing.

Delete the narcissist from all of your contacts

This means EVERYTHING: phone numbers, email addresses, work contact details... everything you have listed. This will remove the ability to reach out where you're pining for them, or feeling down or alone. I can't tell you that this will remove the temptation to reach out when you have the urge to reconnect with them, but it will remove your ability to do so.

Like an addict going cold turkey, initially, you'll crave your substance of choice: your abuser. But, just like an addict, stripping yourself of your addiction and making some behavioral and mental changes sets you on the road to recovery. Take away your ability to obtain your toxic craving by completely deleting every contact method you have.

This is a heart-wrenching yet important and very symbolic step in going no contact.

It took me a good few attempts to do this successfully. At first, I made the choice to block my abuser THEN delete his contacts, knowing full well that if I wanted to speak to him, all I needed to do was search my blocked contacts to obtain his number. This was such a toxic thing to do to myself, and it meant I wasn't fully committing to no contact, which is what is needed in order for it to work: commitment and consistency.

So, as soon as I got his number again, I'd unblock him, get in touch, and allow the entire cycle to be repeated. I just couldn't face the idea of deleting his number altogether; it made everything seem so final.

This is the difficult first step you need to make. If you've not completed this step already, take some time to ask yourself why. What are you holding on for? Don't you deserve better? Take some thinking time and gather your thoughts on what you're clinging to, and why you feel like better isn't an option for you. Hopefully, this will help you muster the courage and move onto the next step. Ideally, you'd change your number to avoid being able to access their number before you head on to the next part of the to-do list.

Block them on everything

I've just told you how I would delete my ex's number, then find it on my block list. This was certainly the case for his phone number, but it wasn't the same for emails and my landline. If my ex wasn't blocked, I know for a fact I'd have answered the calls and messages that I'd have flurrying into my phone.

Remove this possibility by blocking them. Block them on any apps you're messaging them on. Make sure you cover all social media too. I took the step of actually deleting my social media, not only so my ex couldn't contact me but also so I wasn't constantly looking at his page, or mutual friend's pages. For a while, checking up on my ex consumed me. I would wake up and the first thing I would do would be to look at his social media pages, despite it being the last thing I did before I went to bed also. I was eaten up by the thoughts of him moving on, of him hurting someone else, of him having the happy ending that I so desperately wanted. It became an obsession.

Retaining my social media was something I did for a while, and I would block and unblock him and repeat this on a daily basis. It was a relentless cycle where I was at my lowest; I wasn't working, eating, barely sleeping and having my days and nights consumed by him, despite me leaving the relationship and knowing I wanted and deserved more.

The narc will be posting things that will tug at your vulnerable emotions, make you feel sick with jealousy or make you think, 'They weren't that bad'.

Detach from ALL mutual friends, even on social media

Saying farewell to friends you met through your partner may be hard for you, but they will likely have a loyalty to your ex, and your connection will still live on through them.

This may seem harsh, but you will eventually find that freedom is worth it. You will be able to move forward with your life without the flying monkeys acting as chains to your past.

Chapter Four: My First Week of 'No Contact'

The first week of no contact was hellish for me.

I was ill with anxiety, stress, heartache, uncertainty, worries about my family, and wondering if I was ever going to feel okay again. I must point out here that no contact didn't start until a few weeks after I initially left. You'll know yourself that things don't always go to plan or as smoothly as you'd like when it comes to removing yourself from a toxic relationship. I left some contact avenues open, and I found myself in a state of blocking and unblocking my ex. At first, I told myself it was for the children, but I knew deep down I was lying to myself. There was no way we'd be able to be amicable for the kids; that just wasn't him, especially so soon after I'd left him. I was lucky enough that my children were old enough to own their own phones, and they kept in touch with my ex and would arrange to visit him after school and some weekends. I didn't need to leave any door open for my abuser.

After all, that's what I'd done every other time I 'left' the relationship, and I'd always ended up going back. Granted, every other time I left, I bolted to a friend's house, or when I found myself without anyone to rely on, I even used the last of my money to check into a hotel for a couple of days. This time, I'd rented a place. I'd put a deposit down and worked hard to furnish it. This time wasn't like every other time, and I needed to make the most of the strength I'd conjured up to get this far. I needed to capitalize on it to see this through, but it was hard, especially with children having to witness what I was going through.

I was in a mess. I drank too much, slept too much, and became really unhealthy, both mentally and physically. I found that I had overwhelming urges to reach out to my ex, and in order to not give in to these, I needed to take my source of contact away. So, when I felt like typing out a message or text, I threw my phone in a drawer and left the room. I would remove myself as far as I could from my phone, and aim to do something productive, like sort out some paperwork I'd been putting off, or clean, or write a to-do list for what I needed to do for the rest of the week. I would put my focus and energy into *anything* but getting in touch with my ex.

I found that, most of the time at least, that if I took a mental break from thinking about reaching out, when I came back to my phone, I'd have come to my senses somewhat. Of course, for a while, the urge to message him was still there, but logic prevented me from going through with it. I knew that if I did message, I'd be taking steps backward intentionally, and I owed it to myself to not do that. Self-sabotage is a real issue for those who have been in abusive relationships, and it's such an easy pattern to slip into when you feel at an all-time low.

The only way I can really describe my first week of no contact is like a bereavement of some kind. I was mourning the loss of my partner - the person I thought I'd spend my life with, the father of my children. I was grieving the loss of the man I initially met; not the abusive monster he turned out to be, but the kind, engaging, funny person he led me to believe he was at the beginning of the relationship.

I had a lot of sorrow over how things had turned out so differently to how I'd hoped it would. It was tough to comprehend that I'd never, ever be with my ex ever again. At the time, during the first week of no contact, knowing this felt like a punch in the stomach. I was also mourning the time that I'd lost in the relationship, where some of the best years of my life were wasted with someone who didn't respect me, truly love me, or deserve me. I grieved for the young girl who had given such a big chunk of her life to someone who abused her, berated her, mocked her, manipulated her and made her believe she was, and always will be, nothing.

It was a mixture of conflicting emotions that I had to process as best I could. The range of emotions I felt ranged from absolute sorrow to anger to full-blown rage. I would be so upset, which would provoke memories and events that made me angry. I'd then obsess over these hurtful events, which would turn into a rage over how unfair and unjust my situation was. Then I'd collapse into a state of self-pity. This is normal, but at the time, I felt like a complete failure. I just didn't see how I could ever pick myself back up again.

But you do. Eventually, you find yourself in a position that you never imagined possible, where you can function properly and without your abuser consuming your mind. However, during the beginning of going no contact, this seems like it'll never happen. You just need to take it a day at a time.

I would count how long I'd not been thinking about my ex for. For example, if I'd been watching a TV program for half an hour, I'd be proud of the fact that I was allowing my mind to be consumed by that instead of my ex. Of course, thoughts of him would creep back in as soon as I wasn't distracted, and I'll admit that during this period he was mostly all I thought about. But the times where he wasn't at the forefront of my mind became big wins for me.

Eventually, that half-hour of thinking about something else turned into 45 minutes, then 55... It's like a snowball effect, but you need to make the effort to allow other things to enter your thinking in order for it to work. For me, I would watch 'I Survived Evil,' which would often show vile family members or spouses who took abuse to the extreme, and show how the victim escaped and beat their abuser. Lots of the stories would resonate with me, and I would be fully engrossed in their story of heartbreak and triumph, and be inspired by their eventual strength. These shows, although not light-hearted viewing, took my mind elsewhere and made me see how lucky and strong I was capable of being. Often, I'd watch the show and then take to the internet to read more about the survivors of the show and how they overcame such horrible adversity. This, in turn, took my mind away from my own abuser for even longer.

Eventually, I began watching other programs that helped take my mind off of things. I still remember the first time I laughed at a TV show after leaving my relationship and going no contact - I even surprised myself! But it gave me hope. It showed me that the old me was still in there; the one that loved dry comedy, who laughed aloud at the television, the one that had a sense of humor. I was incredibly proud of that seemingly small event.

Chapter Five: How to Maintain the No Contact Rule

A great mindset to have when you're faced with surviving anything in this life is to think of it as a season. You might feel like you aren't blooming in this particular season of your life, but you should remember that you are gaining newfound strength, a renewed sense of self, and energy for your future. It's not easy, and some days can feel like you're taking backward steps instead of forward ones.

You can and will get through this, and happiness and emotional stability is within your reach, I promise. I recall a friend at the time I was struggling with maintaining the no contact rule told me, 'It just takes time'. When I was first told this, it was frustrating; I felt like they had no clue what I was going through and it was just another 'There, there,' phrase to make me feel better. It didn't.

However, as unhelpful to hear as it was at the time, the passing of time really does help you heal. Probably unbeknown to my friend, they were telling me the truth. You just need to find the strength and resolve to maintain no contact, and time will help you slowly shed the heartache, trauma, and pain.

Maintaining the no contact rule is, at its core, a case of mind over matter. You need to shift your mindset to give yourself the best chance possible at making it to the finishing line called healed. This chapter will focus on the way of thinking you need to adopt in order to stay strong enough to get where you deserve to be.

First of all, know that the pain and heartache will eventually fade.

The sheer pain and intensity involved in making the choice to go no contact really does diminish as time goes by. It hurts so much at first simply because you're used to having them as the biggest, most forceful part of your life and they were where most of your hopes and dreams were rooted. You most likely never, ever thought you'd get to this point in the relationship. You may be married. You may have children with this person - both of these things show that you were in it for the long haul. Not having contact with the very person who was your world, who you loved and adored–and likely still do love–feels like a dagger to the stomach. The yearning to be with them, even if it's in an abusive setting, can be utterly overwhelming.

Here's another phrase that you might have heard or been told recently: 'This too will pass'. You're probably thinking, 'I want this feeling to pass right now, I can't deal with it any longer'. It's a hard time to have to force yourself through, but please believe me when I say that you will learn to live without the person you're yearning for. No matter how deeply you love them, or how much you think you can't survive without them, you need to let it sink in that you can be happier once the grief and pain fade - which will happen.

Keep close the fact that hearts heal, wounds eventually close, and hope and energy is once again revived. Have faith in this process, knowing others have walked this path before you, myself included. Hold with you the belief that your happiness will return.

Actively find healthy distractions when you feel close to reconnecting with your abuser

This isn't the advice I was often given during this time to 'get a hobby' or 'join a class' - although both of these things are undeniably good for your soul, I know it's the last thing on your mind during this time. Some days, I couldn't get out of bed because my anxiety and heartbreak were so severe. Eventually, the desire to pick yourself up and consider getting back to old hobbies or making shifts in your lifestyle will come, but whilst you're still fighting the urge to reconnect with your abuser, baby steps are best.

My advice is to find a supportive online group forum - don't feel obliged to participate in discussions if you don't want to though. Just simply read the stories, comments, and advice left by others who are going through the same as you (or who have been through what you're going through.) Just reading through the pain and anguish others are going through will resonate with you and allow you to see that you're not alone. Often, you'll read comments from others who are surviving no contact or trying to maintain no contact. You might feel the urge to then start a dialogue of your own, which will encourage others to offer their thoughts and advice and support.

If you feel the urge to seek out your abuser on social media, instead head to your forum of choice. A simple Google search can find you a whole host of forums dedicated to those struggling with an abusive spouse or ex. Facebook has some really helpful, lifesaving groups you can join, too - seek them all out and you'll find yourself drawn back to a chosen few each time. You may even find some friends there, even if you're not looking for any. This is how I first began my healing journey, and I can't explain how vital it was in my healing process.

As well as this, writing can be a mentally healthy way to distract yourself from heartache and devastation. Write about how you feel, what you want from life, where you want to be in six months time. You can write about the trauma you've endured and keep it somewhere safe to read during times when you feel weak and like you're going to regain contact. Whilst I don't want all of your thoughts to be wasted on your ex, I know the power of getting all of the pain down onto paper. Write it out, type it, or even draft it in the notes section on your phone - whatever way you do it, allow yourself some time to release the inner turmoil you're going through because of your abuser.

Take the time to seek out things that are true, pure and healing

When I find myself constantly dwelling on the hurtful things that I've endured, I shift my train of thought purposefully. I don't try to suppress or block out unhealthy or painful things, I instead simply refocus my thoughts on things that fill me with a sense of happiness, hope, strength, and inspiration. This makes me feel incredibly lucky that I'm alive; albeit heartbroken and a little lost in the world, but often, it's these phases of our life that lead to the best destinations.

I also find that whenever I'm feeling incredibly sorry for myself, and cross the line from being low to becoming self-pitying, I need to reevaluate my way of thinking. One time, when I was in a state of sheer self-indulgence, drinking away my sorrow, I came across a news article about a mother who'd lost her two of her children and partner in a house fire. She was utterly bereft, and after reading the article, I felt incredibly guilty; I wondered to myself, how on earth can she go on? But, she was. She was pregnant, and she was battling through this life-changing, traumatic experience all on her own.

Reading this made me feel a sense of shame, and incredibly guilty. Here I was, tormenting myself over a man who'd broken me, belittled me, emotionally and physically abused me, not leaving the house and self-medicating with alcohol. Then there was this brave woman I read about in the paper who was adamant she was going to stay strong and crush the life she had been blessed with. This gave me a jolt of reality and helped show me how lucky I really was: I was healthy, I had a roof over my head, I was the captain of my own ship.

To summarize, when you're struggling with the thoughts of contacting someone you love, take the time to shift your thoughts. Trust me, even if it takes a little time and persistence, your emotions will follow suit and you will begin to feel better.

Allow yourself to go through periods of hurt and brokenness

Like I mentioned before, I often overstepped the mark from grieving to allowing myself to fall into downright self-pitying and self-indulgent behavior (and not the good kind of self-indulgence.)

It's important to know that you should avoid crossing over that line, but also understand that you do need to endure these periods of pain. Invite them, endure them, work through them, and eventually, you'll be able to put them to bed.

We all have to suffer this part of the painful process. In order to come out of the other side, you need to find your way through the darkness. The grief you're going through is awful, but you need to keep going through the darkness. Allow yourself to submerge right into it – making sure to hold on to the anchor of hope.

The best way to heal from a breakup is to be firm about the "no contact" rule. It's like a Band-Aid that is ripped off – the pain is excruciating at first, but if you focus on healing emotionally and spiritually, your suffering won't be for nothing.

Chapter Six: Triangulation - Yet Another Manipulation Technique

You may have experienced this horrific type of manipulation before - in order to draw you back to them, narcissists will try and create an aura of desirability around themselves. They'll curate the idea of being wanted and adored by many. It can become almost a point of clouded vanity for you to be the number one object of their attention, to attract them away from their growing crowd of admirers. A narcissist will manufacture the illusion of being ultra popular and sought after by surrounding themselves with potential suitors. This can be friends, previous lovers, and also your eventual replacement. Then, the narcissist will purposefully create triangles that encourage rivalry and this will serve to raise their perceived stock or value.

Before I continue with this chapter, I would like to mention the fact that people **do** fall in and out of love all the time; it's a painful fact of life. People can (and do) find new partners, both before and after a relationship ends. People can be deceitful and cheat on one another. I want to be clear; this chapter is not about these everyday occurrences, which I know are painfully unfair and heartbreaking. Rather, this chapter is about a very specific set of actions and patterns that narcissists utilize in order to torture and maintain control of their victims. I mention this because, when I endured the heart-wrenching pain of triangulation, my former friends tried to normalize my abuser's behavior as a part of 'modern dating'; trying to make me jealous by flaunting new partners in my eye-line and making sure I knew he was sought after. 'It's what people do - it's how relationships work,' I was told. Such awful misadvice I was given by people who wanted me to accept this behavior as 'normal'. I wanted to make a point of this before delving any further into this chapter, just to draw a line between the heartache that occurs in 'healthy' break-ups, and the purposeful heartache inflicted upon you in a narcissistic break-up.

Narcissists, like most psychopaths and sociopaths, seek out power and control. They aim to dominate their spouses emotionally, physically, and often, sexually. They do this, as you likely already know, by exploiting vulnerabilities. This is why they utilize the manipulative tactic of love-bombing you with attention and adoration at the beginning of the relationship - the narcissist knows that no matter how strong or confident you may be, being in love, by default, makes you vulnerable. Narcissists don't actually need physical aggression to control you (although this doesn't stop some of them from lashing out anyway). Instead, for narcissists, relationships provide them with the perfect setting to consume their victims by manufacturing an illusion of love. This is why it's so hurtful and emotionally jarring when bystanders say, 'I don't understand - why didn't you just leave?'

Of course, you never entered a relationship with a psychopath to your knowledge - who would? You weren't hoping or expecting to be abused, dehumanized, and criticized. You don't stay in an abusive relationship because you love how it makes you feel. To suggest that what you're going through is your fault is sheer uneducated ignorance by those who suggest you could end your pain by not entering the relationship in the first place. What people fail to realize is that you were tricked into falling in love, which is the most unwavering human bond that can exist. Psychopaths know and utilize this.

So, just how do narcissists maintain such a powerful bond with their victims? One of their most used methods is through triangulation. When I use this term, you may automatically equate it with their next target, but this isn't always the case. Narcs use triangulation frequently to seem in 'high demand' in order to keep you 'obsessed' with them. This can occur with anyone.

They can use your family in their attempt at triangulation, which is arguably the most crushing and frustrating, alongside their use of your own friends against you. They'll also use their own friends and family, which can cause just as much pain, particularly if you were close with their other triangulation victim. Narcs can also bring in a complete stranger to the mix; someone you've never heard of or seen before, but someone the narcissist has likely had waiting in the sidelines.

The narcissist's ability to groom others is unparalleled. They feel a great, intense sense of euphoria when they're able to turn people against each other, more so when it's over competition for them. Narcs will quite happily and easily manufacture situations to make you jealous and question your worth to have them in your life. In a healthy, normal relationship, partners tend to go out of their way to prove that they are honest and trustworthy. Emotionally stable spouses want you to feel safe and secure in the relationship, but a narcissist will do exactly the opposite.

They are forever suggesting that they have other options available to pursue, or they'll prioritize spending time with other people, doing so with the intent that you can never obtain a feeling of peace in the relationship. Of course, they will always deny this, and call you crazy for being so 'paranoid'.

The problem (created with clear purpose by the narc) here is that now you're accustomed to a high level of affection and attention after they first reeled you in, so it feels so jilting, hurtful and confusing when they choose to direct that attention elsewhere. The narc knows this. They'll 'forget' plans they've made with you, and instead they'll perhaps spend time with friends that they always moaned about to you. They'll ignore you to spend more time with other people, even when the narc has stated to you that these people are 'horrible'. They'll manipulatively seek sympathy from an ex when there's a family bereavement or emergency and explain it away by saying they have a 'connection' or 'bond' that you just wouldn't understand. Often, that ex is someone they have had less than glowing things to say about them; they may have told you their ex is unstable, a psychopath or plain crazy. This can make you feel all the more cast aside and confused when they choose to spend time with them.

Seeking hordes of attention, an abundance of sympathy and solace from people who aren't their main victim is a very common tactic of the narc. As a sympathetic and empathetic person, and as their spouse, you (rightfully so) feel that they should be seeking that comfort in you; their partner. You know you've been there to heal them in the past, so why not now? Now, they turn to private friendships or prior relationships that you don't understand'. This part, of course, is shoved in your face.

Technology also makes it so much easier for narcs to manipulate you through triangulation. It can be something as simple as liking a post from an ex, while ignoring your post. They will 'accidentally' upload a photo album, making sure to include the picture where they're embracing their ex (the one they claimed to hate.) Everything's made to look unintentional, and you likely often attribute it to insensitivity at times but make no mistake about this: it's all calculated behavior.

They'll post strategically ambiguous statuses, videos, quotes, songs, and pictures that suggest you might be at risk of 'losing' them. They'll share things that are very intentionally meant to lure in new targets. For example, an inside joke with their new victim kills two birds with one stone; it lures them in and serves to hurt you. Narcs also like to lure back old victims. They may share the song that they once shared with their ex. This again accomplishes two things: it leaves you feeling anxious, unhinged and filled with jealousy. But it also serves to make the 'competing' person feel special. They are systematically grooming others and they are eroding your confidence and sense of self.

The manipulative narcissist will want you to confront them about these things, because they can be seen as, on the surface, minimal. This means that you will appear crazy, psychotic and jealous for even bringing it up. The narcissist will calmly provide you with an excuse for everything and then proceed to blame you. Covert abuse is often frustratingly impossible to prove because it's always so calculated and strategically ambiguous. You can't outright prove that they're communicating with their ex because of something they posted, but you know it deep down.

You still have your intuition, despite the narc trying to cloud that and daze you with anxious emotions. This is how they lay the foundations for crazy-making. Because, really, complaining about social media statuses, comments and posts does *seem* immature and petty. That's exactly how the narcissist wants you to feel.

Narcissists are also highly skilled at surrounding themselves with 'givers' - insecure people who find their own self-worth by taking care of others. This explains why your giving can often seem so insignificant and replaceable throughout the relationship. They will also be sure to voice their love of qualities in others who are nothing at all like you - often the exact opposite of you. The message here is simple: you are not special. You're replaceable. If you don't willingly give them the worshiping they deserve, no worries: they'll always have other sources of that supply. And even if you do give them all of your energy, they'll get bored with you sooner or later. They don't need you in particular - they can get what you're offering anywhere at all. Their crowd of fans will always be there to admire them, making you believe that they really must be someone special. But don't be fooled. Just like you, they'll have an unspoken misery about them, make no mistake.

The final triangulation occurs when the narc makes the choice to abandon you. This is when they'll begin openly and frequently talking about how much the relationship is hurting them, and how they feel unable to deal with your crazy, psychotic behavior anymore. They will probably mention talking to a close friend about the relationship, going into hurtful and confusing details about how their friend agreed that your relationship was toxic and unhealthy. Throughout this, they've likely been blatantly ignoring frantic, panicked messages from you. You'll be hurtfully wondering why they aren't chatting with you - their partner - about these concerns.

The reason for this is that they've already made the decision to end things with you - but not before torturing you. They will only seek advice from people who they know will agree with their points. If you let everything unfold, you'll probably find that the 'friend' they've been talking to about you is their new target.

After the breakup, the narcissist will openly (and loudly) voice how happy they are with their new spouse, whereas most people would feel the need to be very respectful about entering a new relationship so soon after a breakup. And laughably, they fully expect you to be happy for them. If you're not, you are considered bitter and jealous. Which, of course, is what the narcissist will be calling you when you're not over the moon about their behavior.

During this time, the narcissist will then make a post-breakup assessment. If you grovel and beg for them back, they are likely to still find some value in your energy. They will be simultaneously disgusted and euphoric by your behavior. If you lash out and begin exposing their lies, they will do everything in their power to break you emotionally. Should you then come back to them later with an apology, they won't have forgotten your actions towards them; as if you dared talk back to them or 'ruin' them, you'll be a target of their contempt. You've seen too much and you know too much - you've seen the person behind the mask.

This is why they'll wave their new partner in front of your face, posting lots of pictures and declaring their newfound happiness on social media. They want to show how happy and perfect their life is now. It's a final, cruel attempt to drive you to the brink of insanity with triangulation.

The exes who do stay strung to the narcissist's clutches don't understand that they are mere puppets to the narc. Instead, they feel like they are fulfilling their duty as a friend or close confidante - someone who will always be there for them, no matter what life does to get between them. They don't (or don't want to) understand that they are only kept around for when the narc gets bored or needs to use them for something. They are living under the illusion that their relationship with the narc is brilliant, unique, and perhaps misunderstood. When in reality, they are just a pawn that's used for triangulation and manipulation.

You need to protect yourself from this dehumanizing abuse. By knowing what triangulation is, you now have the foundations to deflect it; you know what the narcissist is doing.

Funnily enough, every single time you remove the narcissist from your life, you will find that the yearning and anxiety subsides. Give yourself the opportunity to let the painful feelings go away by not getting dragged into the hurt of triangulation and maintaining no contact.

Triangulation without a doubt leaves long-lasting emotional scars, and it makes you really believe that you're jealous, needy, and insecure. You can start healing those scars by understanding that they were manufactured. No matter how unhinged you acted or how your anxiety prompted you to behave, you were not yourself - you were manipulated into acting this way. The real you is kind and loving, with a great deal of compassion - if you didn't have these things, the narcissist would never have been interested. They took advantage of these great qualities. Understand this in order to heal.

Chapter Seven: My Experiences With Triangulation

When I came to write this chapter, I began to reflect on my personal experiences with triangulation. I then realized I was struggling to pick just one episode of triangulation because there had been so many throughout the relationship!

I think the time that hurt the most was where he eventually ended up in a relationship with the person he was using to 'bait' me. It started when my ex began a new job, and it required him to travel for conferences and meetings. At first, this gave me a sense of relief, as I relished my alone time, and it gave me a break from his dominating presence. However, it was on one of these work trips that he solidified a new relationship with another woman; the same woman he had been triangulating me with for months prior.

It started out by him coming home and talking about this woman from work. He would talk about her quite a lot, more than just your normal co-worker. At that point, I had become wise to his game of trying to make me envious, so whilst it annoyed me that he was relentlessly gushing about a woman from work, I knew he was prone to doing this to get a bite out of me. I thought nothing more of it until I saw messages from her popping up on her phone (or rather, the number saved as 'B' in his phone, which was her first initial - it didn't take much to gather this was her texting him.) Again, nothing criminal in sending a co-worker a text, but the amount they were texting was extreme, and the number of times I woke up in the night to find him texting her was more than I can recall.

I knew if I mentioned this, my ex would just make me out to be a jealous psychopath.

So, as I knew what would happen if I confronted him, I scratched that from my list of options. I needed to find out if something was going on. It was driving me mad. Just as the narcissist wants, pitting the victim against a potential threat turns them into a bundle of fear and anxiety, which turns them irrational. I couldn't find this woman on my ex's list of friends on Facebook, so I initially thought they weren't connected on there. Then it dawned on me: she might have me blocked. In a panic, I created a new Facebook profile to find out, and sure enough, I could see her profile and that she was friends with my husband. Again, there's no crime in that, but why would she block me? She'd never met me, so what could I have done to make her block me?

This sent me into a state of sheer panic. I couldn't think straight, I had no way to prove anything was going on, and I couldn't broach this with my partner as he would humiliate me for 'acting like a psycho'. I was in bits.

My stomach was churning the next time he had to go away for work, as I knew B would be there. They were attending the same conference and sharing the same hotel. I was slowly becoming more and more heartbroken and irrational; I even begged him not to go. I felt sick at the thought of my ex going there with the other woman. Just like the narcissist wants, my anger and hatred was aimed towards their other victim, not the puppet master directly. This suits the narcs needs perfectly; it makes the victim pander to their abusive spouse, all the while the victim is becoming unhinged, which allows the narcissist to paint them out as unstable. It's like the jackpot of narcissistic supply for the abuser.

Of course, my ex did go on the trip. As I frantically messaged him as he was away, he would leave me on 'read'. It hurt all the more to see he had checked into his hotel (via Facebook) but was ignoring my pleading messages.

Eventually, when he did reply that evening, he said he had been busy all day, so he wasn't able to reply, but I could see from B's Facebook that they'd been drinking at the hotel bar. Even more hurtfully, my ex then texted me a picture of his meal that evening, and he managed to catch half of B's face in the frame. It was like a dagger to my heart.

I couldn't eat or sleep whilst he was away, I was in a horrible state of panic. That picture was the last text he sent me before returning home the next evening. When he got back, he went straight to bed and slept right through until the next afternoon, which is what he did when he was hungover. I began to suspect (the quite obvious truth) that my husband didn't go on a business trip - it was a night away with another woman.

Unbeknown to me at the time, he was pitting me and B against each other. He made me have an unhealthy dislike towards her because she was apparently everything I was not; he gushed about the funny things she said and thought she was brilliant because she gave him lots of compliments about how good he was at his job. As I later found out, he was also feeding her his toxic lies by telling B I was psychotic and controlling, and he had her block me on Facebook as I would go crazy if I saw they were friends. He even suggested that she wouldn't be safe if I knew about her existence! He told her that he only stayed with me for the children and that he was afraid of what I'd do if he left.

There was another instance where he brought the other party to our house. This was yet another woman, from another workplace, whom he'd been getting closer to. He yet again tried his best to make me jealous and paranoid about this woman, who he said he'd 'known for years', but it turned out they'd not even worked in the same office for more than a month. He'd befriended her on social media, under the guise that he needed a new gym partner (as she was a real fitness buff). My husband rarely went to the gym, yet he'd told this woman that he would often go with me, but I'd become complacent and refused to go with him any longer - this was an outright lie. I think I've been in two gyms my entire life, and one of those I'm sure I entered by mistake. He also wasn't the gym bunny he was making himself out to be, either; he was using one of her passions to lure her in.

So, as the outgoing, friendly woman she was, she offered to go with my husband and show him around her gym. This then turned into her picking him up from our house, to which my husband would always comment on how much 'get up and go' she had, and his demeanor would also shift when she was around. He became uber friendly, smiley and flirtatious, which was an attempt to make me envious and make her feel flattered.

He made me out to be a lazy, boring and unfriendly spouse to this woman, which is what she saw when she would come to pick him up at 6 am. In reality, I was beaten down, broken and made to feel utterly miserable by my husband. The man she saw - the happy, easy-going, kind man - wasn't the one he was behind closed doors, and it was unbearably frustrating to know this.

There were many other instances of triangulation, and they worked almost every time. Towards the end, they began to work a bit less: I didn't feel the outright burning pain of abandon that I'd felt earlier on in the relationship, but it still certainly hurt. My ex still tried to continue this method of manipulation after the relationship had ended, too. Despite me maintaining no contact and not speaking to him, he'd go out of his way to flaunt his new relationship in front of me. He'd take his new partner to the bar directly opposite my office at work, knowing full well I'd see them sitting there from my office window. My window looked out directly onto the bar, which had outdoor seating that was right in my eye line when I sat at my desk. He'd look up at my office window as he sat there with his newest victim, waiting for me to see them together.

This did still hurt somewhat, but in no way did it feel like a dagger to the heart. At this point, I knew I was going to overcome everything he'd put me through. His grip on me had slipped, and it filled me with pride to know that I could see him with someone else and not let it break me. The effort he went to: securing a new victim, taking them to that particular bar outside of my work, and waiting for me to spot them, was utterly pathetic.

Chapter Eight: I've Broken No Contact - Can No Contact Work the Second Time Around?

Okay - so, you caved in. Either you got in touch with the narcissist, or you allowed them back into your life after they reached out to you.

Let me first of all start by offering you some hope: The no contact rule can, and will, work twice. It can work again whether you were the one to reach out or if you succumbed to the narcs constant chipping away at you. Don't be deterred from doing this again, just because it's not worked for you so far.

Don't let the mental block of thinking, 'I'm not strong enough to stick with this' get in your way - being defeatist will only make sure you're stuck in the abusive cycle forever. To be entirely truthful, the no contact rule can work the third, fourth and fifth time - beyond that even I know it took me a good few attempts to completely cut my abuser off, so I know that no contact can work well past this number. There is a downside, however, which I'd like to cover.

If you failed with this no contact, please don't panic or berate yourself. No contact can work again - but just because it can work again, please don't take it any less seriously as if you only had one shot at implementing it. You need to be accountable for any post-breakup mistakes you make and do your best to avoid repeating the same ones again and again.

So, repeat this mantra: Maintain no contact - zero! No ifs, no buts, or maybe's.

Say the above mantra out loud, even if you think you sound silly or you feel awkward doing so. In fact, if you're in a position to say it right now, give it a go. Even if you don't feel connected to that quote right now, say it. Even if it seems unachievable, hypocritical, or whatever negative spin you put on it, say it aloud.

I know from experience that there is a lot of misleading and damaging information on the internet in regard to 'no contact'. Some self-proclaimed relationship 'experts' will advise the broken-hearted to utilize no contact with the sole intention of reaching out after a set period of time. They say that their ex will have missed them and welcome them back with open arms. This, at best, is sheer game-playing, and at worst utterly damaging to those who are in the abusive cycle. When I first delved into knowing as much as I could about narcissism, I bought into what some of these 'experts' were telling me; *show them what they're missing, and if they don't reach out, re-enter their life with an apology and flatter them with how much you've missed them. This will fix your broken relationship.*

Luckily, I came to my senses before acting on any of this ill-given advice. I had the support of abuse forums and Facebook groups to help guide me, but I'm still shocked at the number of utterly dangerous advice out there. So, if you've broken the NC rule, don't panic and don't blindly follow the damaging advice so many blogs and articles are preaching: stick to logic and forget game playing.

You're trying to separate from a narcissist and the toxic bond you have developed, and perhaps you've gone some time without contacting them or interacting with them in any way. But, then you slipped up. Don't worry. Don't become flustered. It happens - a lot. Rarely does anyone manage to see no contact through on their first time (but they can and have so don't let this fact put you off aiming for that!) You must remember that we are talking about a hugely powerful pattern to break free from here. Some people, maybe yourself included, have been in this kind of situation for their whole lives, with trauma bonding patterns going back to childhood, reinforcing everything they're going through. In this situation, breaking away isn't easy to do at all. Lots of victims slip up and fall back into the trap, so it's really important that you remember not to beat yourself up over it. It's a case of re-establishing your boundaries, putting the no contact rule back in place and going again. It's as simple as that. I'm not saying it's easy - it's not, as you'll already know - but the actions you need to adhere to are simple. It's **simplicity + consistency = breaking free** from the toxic bond. If the no contact rule has been broken, don't overcomplicate it. You've fallen off the horse? Okay. Get back on and try again.

Breaking no contact doesn't mean that all of the work you've done on yourself has been for nothing, either. Breaking the NC rule doesn't erase all the work you've done on yourself. Yes, you've taken a step back (possibly two), but you now know how to take that step forward again. You just need to keep at it. Remember, by going no contact, it means you're really, seriously trying to break out of a pattern that you could have endured your entire life, one that you are basically emotionally addicted to and dependent on to make you feel 'okay'. Making the mistake of breaking no contact isn't the end of the world. In saying that, you also need to be careful not to cut yourself too much slack. I'm a big advocate for not being harsh on yourself, but the voice of addiction is very sneaky, especially when you're bonded to your abuser. It can de-rationalize anything and is massively persuasive. It's important to remember that even a teeny-tiny bit of poison is still poison. To put this in perspective, you don't get cancer from smoking a single cigarette after you've tried to quit cigarettes altogether. You get cancer from repeatedly continuing to smoke after trying to quit, but giving in to your addiction. It's the exact same principle here. One slip up really is not the end of everything, but if those slip-ups turn into a pattern, it'll become a problem.

Take your mistake for what it is and focus on working to do better next time.

If you're repeatedly slipping up and caving into your toxic ex, you may feel overwhelmed and like it's out of your control. It's not, and here are three explanations as to why you keep slipping up; these reasons as to why people break the NC rule are the most common ones, and I'm sure at least one will resonate with you.

Reason #1: People tend to break the no contact rule when they are feeling vulnerable. This can be when you're feeling especially lonely or sad, or it can be when your ex has gotten in touch to say that they're lonely or sad or depressed. The relenting that then happens occurs partly because of our own instinctive humanity and also because of the trauma bond that emotionally ties us to our abuser. Victims who have been so traumatized and emotionally crushed come to depend on the 'happy feelings' that come after abuse, where the abuser is full of sorrow and is all apologetic and everything feels like it's true love again. The victim is used to the emotional and chemical lift that comes from the abuse being stopped. It's natural that, when people in this situation begin to feel especially vulnerable or sad, they want to feel better in the only way they know how to. This was me for so long; I'd return to the relationship just to find some kind of 'happy' no matter what I had to endure to get there. Don't let this be you. The feelings of pain and heartbreak are temporary, no matter how much you feel like they're never-ending. Your mind, spirit, and body found ways to cope during the abuse and they will certainly find ways to cope now that the abuser has gone. It takes a little time to adjust, but you have to let it work itself out because it will. Maintain your patience and think about your self-respect. That's far, far more important to you than temporarily feeling better.

Reason #2: People sometimes break no contact because they feel guilty. They realize their toxic ex is a disordered, deeply miserable person and they feel bad for them. There isn't anything wrong with that in normal circumstances - empathy is a great trait to have. But it's also dangerous when you're in the clutches of a narcissist. You can still feel pity for your abuser, but not at your own expense. Part of engaging in self-care is not engaging in situations where you are being hurt, no matter what. You can pity a person while at the same time knowing that there is nothing you can do to help or save them. This is how you need to view your ex if you find yourself giving in to guilt. Yes, they are a victim of a miserable existence - but that's their own doing. Yes, it is a terrible shame. There is nothing you or anyone else can do; only the narcissist can change the components within them that make them live a life of manipulation and hurt. And the chances of that happening are close to zero. No matter how you feel, and regardless of what your abuser says, it's not possible to help them. It isn't possible to help *anyone* who doesn't understand that there is a huge problem and you can't force them to have the desire to fix it.

Reason #3: People can break no contact out of fear. Victims tend to go into a state of panic when they realize the relationship could really be over this time - despite this being the end goal of no contact. This way of thinking goes to show just how messed up the narcissist makes you; you're doubting your decision based off of a fear they've instilled into you. People can experience a fear that the narc no longer cares about them, or they endure sheer panic if they feel their abuser will find a new person to care about. Once out of the relationship, it's natural for the victim to worry excessively about what their ex is doing or who they're talking to. The anxiety this induces often means that the victim will reach out to the narcissist to find out what they've been up to.

If you feel this way, it's important to remember that people will do what they want to do, and there's no way for you to control that. You only stress yourself out worrying about things you can't control, which is unhealthy. What is in your power, however, is to be able to get out of the situation, learn that you don't deserve to be treated in such an awful way, and move on.

***

There are lots of relationships out there where there is a real fundamental problem, such as cheating or lack of communication. One spouse perhaps cheats on the other constantly, and as you'd expect, the other one doesn't like it one bit - who would? It's incredibly hurtful. It's without a doubt disrespectful. But, often, instead of ending the relationship with the person who's cheating - who clearly cannot be faithful for their own reasons - the faithful partner fights and insists that the cheater repent and change.

The faithful spouse will attempt to control the cheater's movements, whereabouts, friends, and daily life in an effort to stop them from cheating once again. This is totally understandable and relatable from an emotional standpoint, but you can admit, it's not healthy at all. It's also incredibly bad for any children involved and it hurts more than just the two people in the relationship. The reason I'm mentioning this is that lots of people have a problem with the way their partner behaves, but instead of ending the relationship, they stay and try to control the person and *force* them to change. So, looking at this situation from a third-person perspective, you should be able to see that the healthy thing to do is to end the relationship. With the two options being to end the toxic relationship or keep enduring it and hoping it'll get better, the latter of the two options is soul-destroying.

The narc won't be motivated to change for their spouse or their kids or their mother or father or anybody else, and they'll never take pleas for them to change seriously. It's not worth your time, energy or any of your precious mind space to let them fool you with false promises of 'change'. Narcissists can be truly awful and sneaky and morally wrong and as abusive that they want to be - and they will be. But you don't have to put up with it.

And that's essentially what no contact is all about. Not putting up with it anymore. It's your way of claiming back your power and standing up to the person who's hurt and suppressed you for so long. It's not a punishment to the narcissist, it's something you owe to yourself to do. You have to keep in mind that it has no end. There is no '21 day rule' here. I read somewhere that you only need to do no contact for as many months as you've been with them in years; for example, if you've been with your partner for 2 years, your no contact period is 2 months. This is not how you truly escape and heal from an abusive relationship - this is how you stay in an abusive relationship and prolong your agony.

To be matter of fact about no contact, it's essentially the stopping of your association with a person who has demonstrated that they are not someone whose behavior is that of a loving, caring and decent spouse. Because of this, you've rightly chosen not to tolerate it. Try to keep this logical way of looking at it at the forefront of your mind; you need logic to pull you back from your trauma bonded emotions at this point. It can be incredibly hard to keep no contact, because of the addictive, highly dependent nature of the relationship, but try to cut through the emotional fog with logic and rationale.

There are things you can do to exercise the feeling of contacting your ex without giving in. Write a letter to them, but don't send it. After you've poured your heart out, you can even destroy the letter - it could be cathartic for you. You could write a list of things you want to accomplish, of hopes and dreams you have, and hopefully jotting these down will make you realize you can achieve them, but not if you're with a narcissist. You can also distract yourself so you divert your mind onto other things other than the narc. You could go for a run, walk your dog, play video games, catch a movie alone, do something that scares you, visit a restaurant that's just opened, go to an art class, start new hobbies... the list of nourishing things you can do is endless. The most important thing is to acknowledge your feelings for what they are and allow them to work themselves out without involving the narcissist. You really can't work on your own feelings and emotions with someone around who is unable and unwilling to understand that you even *have* feelings.

The only thing that will happen is predictable: your feelings will be ignored and you will remain unhappy and unfulfilled. No contact is about breaking that toxic pattern, and it takes work and effort and a lot of trudging through the pain, but it is possible. Don't give in!

You might have picked up that I've not mentioned how the narcissist reacts when you break the no contact rule. That's because it doesn't matter - you shouldn't spend your time focusing on the narcissist right now. They will react how they always react to injury. There's nothing new here.

What's really important here is how **you** feel and how **you** react to it. The narc may step up their efforts to get your attention back once you reestablish the no contact rule, but that's also pretty predictable. You already know how the narcissist acts and reacts;

it's never anything new. It's far, far more important to figure out *your* feelings. Let the narcissist worry about their own feelings instead of you.

Chapter Nine: Moving Forward

You've either chosen this book because you're looking to go no contact with your abuser, or because you're currently implementing no contact and needed some support and encouragement to aid you through the journey. I hope it's been of use as a source of inspiration and support.

I know that this period of your life is painful and seemingly never-ending, but if you take one thing away from this book, it's that breaking the chains **is** possible. I can't lie and say it's easy or immediate, but it's within your remit to do, no matter your situation or circumstances. You can do it because you have to do it. I want to give you some affirmations that helped me during this emotionally turbulent time, and I hope they'll help you when you need some support, too. Each affirmation is something that you should say aloud if you can. With each one, I've given a little paragraph of context to help you understand the meaning behind each one, and you can apply it to your own situation.

Affirmation #1. Every second of my silence is protection against psychological abuse towards me.

Every time you make the conscious choice not to check up on, respond to or reach out towards your abusive ex, you're showing yourself that you value yourself, your time, and your absolute right not to be subjected to such toxic mistreatment. You are protecting yourself from traumatizing situations and perhaps even violence that would only further re-traumatize you. You're removing yourself from the abusive cycle. The abusive cycle can only ever expose you to more pain and hopelessness. You have bravely escaped from that abusive cycle – don't allow yourself to walk right back into that again. It does get more and more difficult to leave every time you do.

Affirmation #2. As a human being, I have a right to be free from abuse.

You are just like any other human being. You reserve the right to live a life free of abuse, just like everyone else.

Affirmation #3. I am stronger than an abuser's attempts to bully me.

With narcissistic relationships often forging a traumatic bond, you may find that you're hearing your abuser's voice or are being shamed or coerced back into the relationship. Survivors of any abuse are often left reeling from the relentless bullying behavior of their ex. Stalking and harassing aren't uncommon, and the toxic ex will even go as far as to flaunt their new source of supply to them as a way to goad you into a response. Allow this affirmation to remind you that the abuser's tactics can't work on you as much if you are prepared to prioritize your strength, future, and freedom over their attempts to provoke you. Of course, the manipulation and bullying may hurt, but where there is a strong will, the narcissist has a job on his hands to break that.

Affirmation #4. I will defend myself.

That may mean getting a restraining order, changing your number or even moving house, you need to do whatever you need to in order to protect yourself from the narc's manipulation and abuse on your journey. You don't deserve to be abused, in any way, shape or form. You can even seek support from local domestic violence or abuse groups, where you can meet other survivors in person. Find out where these take place and at what time, even if you don't feel ready to go just yet. They are a huge source of support, however, so I do recommend plucking up the courage to go.

Affirmation #5. I will keep going.

No matter how difficult it feels, you need to keep going. If you do make a mistake, remember that all is not lost. How do you beat anything in life? You certainly don't let imperfection or mistakes stop you from progressing on your quest. You don't quit. If you happened to fall off the wagon and broke NC, don't fall into the trap of self-judgment. Get back on the wagon!

Affirmation #6. I deserve more in this life than to be abused and degraded.

When you're in the clutches of an abusive relationship, you're not in a normal, healthy, reciprocal relationship. You are essentially an emotional punching bag for an unstable and toxic person. They take all of their flaws, insecurities, their internal toxicity and spew it out onto you. During the relationship, you were taught by your abuser to simply accept this as a part of being in a relationship with them. Not any more. You deserve more.

Affirmation #7. My mental and emotional health is number one priority now.

Be sure to engage in lots of self-care during no contact. This means you need to be checking in with yourself throughout the day to make sure that you're thinking healthy thoughts, not being self-destructive, and making sure that you're correcting any negative self-talk. Take care of yourself, and please don't be afraid to seek out professional support if things are getting too much for you.

Affirmation #8. My success and happiness will be their karma.

Live your life and aim to lessen your focus on what the narc is doing, who they are seeing or what toxic things they're doing to others. Allow the narcissist to gather at their own pace what happens when you abuse and try to destroy a decent person; they will rise from the ashes, and their strength will carry them towards the happy and fulfilled life they deserve. The narc on the other hand, well, they'll keep being who they are and living with the emotional void they so happily fill with others' misery.

***

And this draws a close to this book. I do hope it's helped you in some way, inspired you, given you new things to think about and offered you some words of comfort along the way.

Do let me know if this has been beneficial for you; you can leave a review, and if you'd like to offer up a little of your own story with it, that would be unbelievably valuable to someone who reads it who's in an abusive relationship.

Here's to being stronger than you ever thought you could be.

Made in the USA
Las Vegas, NV
16 September 2022

55403128R00049